MEXICAN FIESTA
RECIPES

pil

Publications
International Ltd.

Pictured on the front cover: Mexican Pizza *(page 22)*.
Pictured on the back cover: Mexican Steak Tacos *(page 33)*.

ISBN-13: 978-1-4127-2616-0
ISBN-10: 1-4127-2616-6

Manufactured in China.

8 7 6 5 4 3 2 1

Microwave Cooking: Microwave ovens vary in wattage. Use the cooking times as guidelines and check for doneness before adding more time.

Contents

Breakfast Burritos, page 14

Ortega Story   6

Bringing families to the dinner table for more than 100 years

Breakfast & Brunch   8

Wake up your taste buds with these lively dishes

Snacks & Starters   16

Start the party with a fiesta of flavors

Entrées   32

Have a celebration every day of the week with these exciting, authentic Mexican meals

Side Dishes   56

Simple, sensational, south-of-the-border side dishes

Crunchy Mexican Side Salad, page 88

Soups & Salads   72

Hearty, zesty creations perfect as meal starters, entrées, or light lunches

Index   94

Mexican Steak Tacos, page 33

For more than 100 years, Ortega has been committed to family mealtime by providing families with authentic, high-quality products to make a Mexican meal. It all started with Mama Ortega, who took pride in making homemade dishes for her husband and 13 children. With this Ortega Recipe book, we share that tradition with you, helping you make great food and memorable family mealtimes.

Before you head back to the store, make sure you clip out the money-saving coupons in this book. You'll save up to $4.00 on your favorite Ortega products. We hope you enjoy sampling Ortega's rich heritage and specially selected recipes. May it inspire endless happy meals around your own family table.

MAMA ORTEGA

The 150-year Ortega tradition all started with Maria Conception Jacinta Dominguez Ortega, or as we like to call her, Mama.

In the 1800s, Mama and her beloved family lived in a small three-room adobe, common to the Spanish settlements of the time. Inside the thick adobe walls, Mama Ortega created a loving home for her 13 children (yes, 13!) centered around the tiny kitchen. With all those kids to feed, dinner was a major feat indeed.

From her small charcoal-burning stove, Mama Ortega whipped up memorable meals her family loved. Everything for each meal was homegrown, handpicked, and handmade. From the juicy red tomatoes for her sauces to the corn she patted into mouthwatering tortillas, everything Mama lovingly prepared for her family was fresh. Each dish was special. And like today, meals were a time for Mama and her family to come together, enjoy good food and entertain each other with stories of their day. Home-cooked meals have a way of bringing people together like that.

EMILIO C. ORTEGA

Mama's memorable cooking did more than just bring her family together. It was in Mama's kitchen that her 11th child, Emilio, established the Ortega Chile Packing Company. Yep, the first commercial food operation in the state of California was created in the same place Mama created all those unforgettable meals. It may be 150 years later, but we're still inspired by Mama's cooking, and we hope you will be too.

Enjoy the helpful recipe tips and ideas. Find a variety of Mexican recipes—from traditional dishes like those Mama Ortega prepared, to more contemporary favorites.

Break
&

fast Brunch

Mexican Omelette

4 eggs
¼ cup half and half
1 teaspoon dried oregano leaves
½ teaspoon salt
⅛ teaspoon pepper
2 tablespoons butter or margarine
1 (13-ounce) container ORTEGA Salsa & Cheese Bowl
¼ cup ORTEGA Diced Green Chiles
Chopped tomatoes, sour cream and chopped cilantro

MIX eggs, half and half, oregano and salt and pepper with fork.

COAT heated pan with butter. Add egg mixture and spread over bottom of pan. When egg mixture thickens, spread with Salsa & Cheese and chiles. Fold over.

TOP omelette with tomatoes, sour cream and cilantro.

Breakfast Tacos

6 ounces breakfast sausage

1 can (16 ounces) ORTEGA Refried Beans

1 tablespoon butter or margarine

8 eggs, lightly beaten

12 ORTEGA Taco Shells, warmed

2 cups mild Cheddar cheese

2 cups chopped tomato

2 cups chopped green bell pepper

2 cups ORTEGA Salsa, any variety

BROWN sausage in a large skillet until no longer pink; drain. Stir in beans; heat for 3 to 4 minutes. Remove from skillet; keep warm.

MELT butter in a medium skillet over medium heat. Add eggs; cook, stirring constantly, for 3 to 4 minutes or until eggs are of desired consistency.

FILL taco shells with sausage mixture and egg mixture. Top with cheese, tomato, bell pepper and salsa.

Breakfast Empanadas

3 cups plus 2 teaspoons vegetable oil

2 Spanish chorizo links (spicy dried pork sausage; 6 to 8 ounces), casings removed

1 onion, chopped

1 pound boiling potatoes (such as Yukon Gold), peeled and shredded

Salt and black pepper to taste

½ cup ORTEGA Diced Jalapeños

2 plum tomatoes, seeded and chopped

½ teaspoon ground cumin

¼ cup finely chopped
   cilantro

⅓ cup grated queso blanco
   or Monterey Jack cheese

8 frozen empanada or
   turnover wrappers,
   thawed

1 jar (16 ounces) ORTEGA
   Salsa, any variety
   Sour cream (optional)

HEAT 2 teaspoons oil in a
12-inch nonstick skillet over
moderately high heat until hot
but not smoking; cook chorizo
and onion, stirring until onion
is softened. Add potatoes and
salt and pepper. Cook, covered,
stirring occasionally until
potatoes begin to turn golden
brown, about 6 minutes. Stir in
jalapeños, tomatoes and cumin.

TRANSFER to a bowl and cool
completely. Stir in cilantro,
cheese and additional salt and
pepper to taste. Roll out each
empanada wrapper into a 6-inch
round on a floured surface. Put
about ⅓ cup filling in center of
each wrapper and form filling
into a log. Moisten wrapper
edges with a finger dipped in
water. Fold each wrapper over
filling to form a half-moon.
Press down around filling to
force out air. Seal by pressing
edges together firmly with a
fork. Heat remaining 3 cups oil
in a deep 12-inch skillet over
moderate heat until hot but not
smoking. Fry empanadas in
3 batches, gently turning, until
golden brown, about 3 minutes.
Transfer empanadas to paper
towels to drain. Serve with salsa
and sour cream, if desired.

NOTE

Empanadas may be filled one day ahead
and chilled in one layer on a lightly floured plate,
covered. Reseal edges if necessary.

Tortilla Scramble with Salsa

8 eggs

¼ cup heavy whipping cream or half and half

1 tablespoon butter

3 tablespoons ORTEGA Salsa, any variety

1 cup broken ORTEGA Taco Shells

½ cup Cheddar cheese, grated

Tortilla chips, chopped parsley and salsa (optional)

COMBINE eggs and heavy cream in mixing bowl. Beat with wire whisk.

MELT butter in heavy skillet. Add egg mixture and stir in 3 tablespoons salsa. Scramble eggs until they begin to set. Add broken taco shells and cheese, stirring to mix.

DIVIDE egg mixture and place on individual plates.

TOP with tortilla chips, parsley and salsa, if desired.

Breakfast Burritos

½ pound (8 ounces) ground sausage
1 large potato, peeled and grated
1 package (8-inch) ORTEGA Soft Flour Tortillas
4 eggs
1 jar ORTEGA Diced Green Chiles
1 jar ORTEGA Salsa, any variety
1 large tomato, diced
½ cup grated Cheddar cheese
Salt and black pepper
Salsa (optional)

COOK sausage in skillet; add potatoes. Cook until brown. Drain fat.

WARM tortillas according to package directions. Cook and scramble eggs.

DIVIDE eggs, sausage mixture, chiles, salsa, tomato and cheese evenly among tortillas.

SEASON to taste with salt and pepper.

FOLD tortillas and serve immediately. Top with additional salsa, if desired.

Snacks &

Starters

Mexican Tortilla Stacks

½ cup **ORTEGA Salsa, any variety, divided**

¼ cup **sour cream**

½ cup **finely chopped cooked chicken**

8 **(8-inch) ORTEGA Soft Flour Tortillas**

½ cup **prepared guacamole**

⅓ cup **ORTEGA Refried Beans**

6 **tablespoons (1½ ounces) shredded Cheddar cheese**

Sour cream and chopped cilantro (optional)

HEAT oven to 350°F. Mix ¼ cup salsa, sour cream and chicken in small bowl.

PLACE 2 tortillas on ungreased cookie sheet; spread with salsa-chicken mixture. Spread 2 more tortillas with guacamole and place on top of salsa-chicken mixture.

MIX refried beans with remaining ¼ cup salsa; spread onto 2 more tortillas and place on top of guacamole. Top each stack with remaining 2 tortillas; sprinkle with cheese.

BAKE 8 to 10 minutes until cheese is melted and filling is hot.

TOP with sour cream and cilantro, if desired. Cut each stack into 8 wedges.

TIP

Prepared guacamole can be found in the refrigerated or frozen food sections at most supermarkets.

Chile 'n' Cheese Spirals

MAKES 24 APPETIZERS

4 ounces cream cheese, softened

1 cup (4 ounces) shredded Cheddar cheese

1 can (4 ounces) ORTEGA Diced Green Chiles

3 green onions, sliced

½ cup chopped red bell pepper

1 can (2.25 ounces) chopped olives

4 (8-inch) ORTEGA Soft Flour Tortillas

ORTEGA Salsa, any variety

COMBINE cream cheese, Cheddar cheese, chiles, green onions, red pepper and olives in medium bowl.

SPREAD ½ cup cheese mixture on each tortilla; roll up. Wrap each roll in plastic wrap; chill for 1 hour.

REMOVE plastic wrap; slice each roll into 6 (¾-inch) pieces. Serve with salsa for dipping.

NOTE

Chile 'n' Cheese Spirals can be made ahead and kept in the refrigerator for one to two days.

Puffy Tex-Mex Pillows

½ **pound (8 ounces) ground beef**
½ **cup diced red bell pepper**
¼ **cup diced onion**
1 **medium tomato, diced**
1 **cup canned black beans, rinsed and drained**
½ **cup frozen corn, thawed**
¼ **cup water**
1 **package (1.25 ounces) ORTEGA Taco Seasoning Mix**
1 **package (17¾ ounces) frozen puff pastry sheets, thawed according to package directions**
½ **cup plus 1 tablespoon shredded Cheddar cheese**
¼ **cup water**
ORTEGA Salsa, any variety (optional)

COOK beef, bell pepper and onion in large skillet over medium heat about 5 minutes or until beef is no longer pink, stirring to break up pieces.

DRAIN. Add tomato, beans, corn, water and seasoning; cook 2 to 3 minutes, stirring occasionally. Transfer to medium bowl; set aside to cool slightly.

PREHEAT over to 400°F. Unfold pastry sheets on lightly floured surface. Roll each pastry sheet into 12-inch square with lightly floured rolling pin. Cut each sheet into 9 (4-inch) squares. Place about ¼ cup meat filling in center of each pastry square; sprinkle each with 1 tablespoon cheese.

MOISTEN edges of filled squares with water. Place remaining pastry squares on top of filled squares and press edges together with fork to seal. Place on ungreased baking sheet. Bake 10 to 12 minutes or until golden brown. Serve with salsa, if desired.

ORTEGA® Snack Mix

3 cups lightly salted peanuts

3 cups corn chips

3 cups bite-size square
   wheat cereal

2 cups lightly salted pretzels

1 package (1.25 ounces)
   ORTEGA Taco Seasoning
   Mix

¼ cup (½ stick) butter or
   margarine, melted

COMBINE peanuts, corn chips, wheat cereal, pretzels, seasoning mix and butter in large bowl. Toss well to coat. Store in airtight container or zipper-type plastic bag.

TIP

Think ORTEGA® Snack Mix the next time you need a hostess gift or something special for a teacher or friend. It tosses together in minutes and is always a hit. Place the mix in a cellophane bag tied with a ribbon with the recipe card attached. Or, consider packaging it in a decorative tin.

Mexican Pizza

½ pound (8 ounces) ground beef

¾ cup water

1 package (1.25 ounces) ORTEGA Taco Seasoning Mix

1 can (16 ounces) ORTEGA Refried Beans, divided

1 package ORTEGA Tostada Shells

2 cups (8 ounces) shredded Nacho & Taco blend cheese, divided

Shredded lettuce, sliced olives, sliced avocado, chopped cilantro, sliced green onions, chopped tomatoes and sour cream (optional)

BROWN beef; drain. Stir in water and seasoning mix. Bring to a boil. Reduce heat to low; cook, stirring occasionally, for 5 to 6 minutes or until mixture is thickened.

SPREAD 2 tablespoons beans on each tostada shell. Top with ½ cup meat mixture and ¼ cup cheese. Broil for 1 to 2 minutes, or until cheese is melted. Garnish with desired toppings.

TIP

Have family and guests create their own pizzas with the additional toppings provided.

ORTEGA® 7-Layer Dip

1 can (16 ounces) ORTEGA Refried Beans

1 package (1.25 ounces) ORTEGA Taco Seasoning Mix

1 container (8 ounces) sour cream

1 container (8 ounces) refrigerated guacamole

1 cup (4 ounces) shredded Cheddar cheese

1 cup ORTEGA Salsa, any variety

1 can (4 ounces) ORTEGA Diced Green Chiles

2 large green onions, sliced Tortilla chips

COMBINE beans and seasoning mix in small bowl. Spread bean mixture in 8-inch square baking dish.

TOP with sour cream. Continue layering dip with guacamole, cheese, salsa and chiles, finishing with a layer of green onions. Serve with chips.

NOTE

Dip can be prepared and refrigerated up to two hours before serving.

Mexican Roll-Ups

MAKES 70 ROLL-UPS

2 packages (3 ounces each) cream cheese, softened
¾ cup sour cream
1 package (15.2 ounces) ORTEGA Soft Taco Kit
1 can (4 ounces) ORTEGA Diced Green Chiles, drained
¾ cup finely shredded Cheddar cheese
20 (2½×⅜-inch) roasted red pepper strips

BEAT together cream cheese, sour cream and seasoning mix from Soft Taco Kit until smooth. Stir in green chiles and Cheddar cheese.

SPREAD 3 tablespoons cream cheese mixture evenly over each tortilla from kit. Place 2 red pepper strips in center of each tortilla; roll up and wrap in plastic wrap.

CHILL at least 3 hours.

CUT each roll-up into 7 (¾-inch) slices.

SERVE with taco sauce from kit for dipping.

TIP

Roasted red pepper strips can be purchased in 16-ounce jars in the condiment section at most supermarkets.

Smokey Chipotle Party Dip

MAKES 2¼ CUPS DIP

¾ cup sour cream

¾ cup mayonnaise

¾ cup ORTEGA Salsa, any variety

1 package (1.25 ounce) ORTEGA Smokey Chipotle Taco Seasoning Mix

Chopped tomatoes, chopped cilantro, chopped olives and shredded Cheddar cheese

Blue corn tortilla chips

COMBINE all ingredients except chips; stir until blended.

SPREAD dip in shallow serving dish or pie plate and sprinkle with tomatoes, cilantro, olives or cheese, if desired. Serve with tortilla chips.

NOTE

This flavorful dip is ready to go as soon as you make it, but can also be refrigerated and made up to two days before serving.

ORTEGA® Nachos

1 can (16 ounces) ORTEGA Refried Beans, heated

4 cups (4 ounces) tortilla chips

1½ cups (6 ounces) shredded Monterey Jack cheese

¼ cup ORTEGA Sliced Jalapeños

ORTEGA Salsa, any variety, sliced green onions, guacamole, sliced olives, chopped cilantro and sour cream (optional)

PREHEAT broiler.

SPREAD beans over bottom of large ovenproof platter or 15×10×1-inch jellyroll pan. Arrange chips over beans. Top with cheese and jalapeños.

BROIL for 1 to 1½ minutes or until cheese is melted. Top with salsa, green onions and other garnishes, if desired.

ORTEGA® Hot Poppers

1 can (3½ ounces) ORTEGA
Whole Jalapeños, drained
1 cup (4 ounces) shredded
Cheddar cheese
1 package (3 ounces) cream
cheese, softened
¼ cup chopped cilantro
½ cup all-purpose flour
2 eggs, lightly beaten
2 cups cornflake cereal,
crushed
Vegetable oil
ORTEGA Salsa, any
variety, and sour cream

CUT jalapeños lengthwise into halves; remove seeds.

BLEND cheeses and cilantro in small bowl. Place 1 to 1½ teaspoons cheese mixture into each jalapeño half; chill for 15 minutes or until cheese is firm.

DIP each jalapeño in flour; shake off excess. Dip in eggs; coat with cornflake crumbs.

ADD vegetable oil to 1-inch depth in medium skillet; heat over high heat for 1 minute. Fry jalapeños; turning frequently with tongs, until golden brown on all sides. Remove from skillet; drain on paper towels. Serve with salsa and sour cream.

Ent

Mexican Steak Tacos

MAKES 2 SERVINGS

1 (3.5-ounce) boil-in-bag, long-grain rice

2 teaspoons ground cumin

1 teaspoon garlic powder

1 teaspoon ORTEGA Taco Sauce

1 tablespoon ORTEGA Salsa, any variety

¼ teaspoon salt

1 pound sirloin steak
   Nonstick cooking spray

1 can diced tomatoes

1 can (4 ounces) ORTEGA Diced Green Chiles

4 ORTEGA Taco Shells

4 lime wedges
   Sour cream (optional)

COOK rice. Combine cumin, garlic powder, taco sauce, salsa and salt. Rub mixture over both sides of steak.

SPRAY a broiler pan with cooking spray. Place steak on pan. Broil steak for 4 minutes on each side or until desired degree of doneness. Cut steak into thin slices.

COMBINE rice, tomatoes and chiles. Place mixture in shells.

TOP rice mixture with beef slices. Squeeze juice from limes over beef. Top with sour cream, if desired.

Bean and Cheese Burrito

—

1 can (16 ounces) ORTEGA Refried Beans

1 can (4 ounces) ORTEGA Diced Green Chiles

½ teaspoon cumin

1 teaspoon garlic

1 cup chopped red onion

2 tablespoons lime juice

1 package (1.25 ounces) ORTEGA Burrito Seasoning

4 (8-inch) ORTEGA Soft Flour Tortillas

4 tablespoons shredded Cheddar cheese

Nonstick cooking spray

ORTEGA Salsa, any variety, and sour cream

PREHEAT oven to 400°F.

PREPARE filling by mixing beans, chiles, cumin, garlic, onion, lime juice and burrito seasoning.

ASSEMBLE burrito by spooning ½ cup bean filling into center of each tortillas and top with one tablespoon Cheddar cheese. Fold in ends, and then sides.

PLACE burritos seam side down on baking sheets that have been sprayed with cooking spray. Bake for 20 to 25 minutes until golden brown.

SERVE with salsa and sour cream.

Arroz con Pollo

4 slices bacon

1½ pounds (about 6) boneless, skinless chicken breasts

1 cup (1 small) chopped onion

1 cup (1 small) chopped green bell pepper

2 large cloves garlic, finely chopped

2 cups long-grain rice

1 jar (16 ounces) ORTEGA Salsa, any variety

1¾ cups chicken broth

1 cup tomato sauce

1 teaspoon salt

½ teaspoon ground cumin

Chopped parsley

COOK bacon in large skillet over medium heat until crispy; remove from skillet. Crumble bacon; set aside. Add chicken to skillet; cook, turning frequently, for 5 to 7 minutes or until golden on both sides. Remove from skillet; keep warm. Discard all but 2 tablespoons drippings from skillet.

ADD onion, bell pepper and garlic; cook for 3 to 4 minutes or until crisp-tender. Add rice; cook for 2 to 3 minutes. Stir in salsa, chicken broth, tomato sauce, salt and cumin. Bring to a boil. Place chicken over rice mixture; reduce heat to low. Cover. Cook for 20 to 25 minutes or until most of moisture is absorbed and chicken is no longer pink in center. Sprinkle with bacon and parsley.

ORTEGA® Fiesta Bake

2 pounds ground beef
½ cup chopped onion
¾ cup ORTEGA Salsa, any
   variety
1 package (1.25 ounces)
   ORTEGA Taco Seasoning
   Mix
¼ cup water
1 cup whole kernel corn
1 can (2¼ ounces) sliced
   olives, drained
1 package (8½ ounces) corn
   muffin mix
1 large egg
⅓ cup milk
1 cup (4 ounces) shredded
   Cheddar cheese
1 can (4 ounces) ORTEGA
   Diced Green Chiles

PREHEAT oven to 350°F.

COOK beef and onion in large skillet until beef is browned; drain. Stir in salsa, seasoning mix and water. Cook over low heat for 5 to 6 minutes or until mixture thickens; stir in corn and olives. Spoon into 8-inch square baking dish.

COMBINE muffin mix, egg and milk until smooth; stir in cheese and chiles. Spread over meat mixture.

BAKE for 30 to 35 minutes or until corn topping is golden brown.

Fiesta Beef Enchiladas

6 ounces ground beef

¼ cup sliced green onions

1 teaspoon fresh minced or bottled garlic

1 cup (4 ounces) shredded Mexican cheese blend or Cheddar cheese, divided

¾ cup chopped tomato, divided

½ cup frozen corn, thawed

⅓ cup cooked white or brown rice, cold

½ cup black beans

¼ cup ORTEGA Salsa, any variety

6 (6- to 7-inch) corn tortillas

2 sheets (20×12 inches) heavy-duty foil, generously sprayed with nonstick cooking spray

½ cup ORTEGA Enchilada Sauce

½ cup sliced romaine lettuce leaves

PREHEAT oven to 375°F. Brown ground beef in large nonstick skillet over medium-heat, stirring to separate meat. Drain and discard fat. Add green onions and garlic; cook and stir 2 minutes.

COMBINE meat mixture, ¾ cup cheese, ½ cup tomato, corn, rice, black beans and salsa; mix well. Spoon mixture down center of tortillas. Roll up; place, seam side down, on foil sheet, three to a sheet. Spoon enchilada sauce evenly over enchiladas.

DOUBLE fold sides and ends of foil to seal packets, leaving head space for heat circulation. Place packets on baking sheet.

BAKE 15 minutes or until hot. Remove from oven; open packets. Sprinkle with remaining ¼ cup cheese; seal packet. Bake 10 minutes more. Transfer contents to serving plates; serve with lettuce and remaining ¼ cup tomato.

Turkey Tacos

1 tablespoon vegetable oil

1 small onion, sliced

1 small red or green bell pepper, sliced

1 pound boneless, skinless turkey breast, cut into strips

¾ cup water

1 package (1.25 ounces) ORTEGA Taco Seasoning Mix

2 tablespoons sour cream

1 package ORTEGA Taco Shells, warmed
   Shredded Mexican cheese blend, chopped tomato, shredded lettuce and Ortega Taco Sauce

HEAT vegetable oil in large skillet over medium-high heat. Add onion and bell pepper; cook, stirring occasionally, for 3 to 4 minutes or until vegetables are tender. Add turkey; cook, stirring occasionally, for 4 to 5 minutes or until turkey is no longer pink.

ADD water and seasoning mix. Heat until thickened, stirring often. Stir in sour cream.

FILL taco shells with turkey mixture. Top with cheese, tomato, lettuce and taco sauce.

BBQ Chicken Tacos

1 package ORTEGA Taco
   Shells, heated
1 container (2 pounds)
   prepared shredded
   chicken in barbeque
   sauce, warmed

1 cup (8 ounces) prepared
   coleslaw
   Shredded Monterey Jack
   cheese (optional)

FILL taco shells with chicken.
Top with coleslaw and cheese, if
desired.

TIP

For a refreshing fruit side dish, combine
two tablespoons orange juice, one tablespoon each
lemon juice and honey and one teaspoon Dijon-style
mustard in a blender. Slowly add $1/3$ cup vegetable oil
through hole in lid; blend until thickened.
Toss with assorted fruit.

Fajita Celebration

1 jar (16 ounces) ORTEGA Salsa, any variety
¼ cup vegetable oil, divided
2 tablespoons chopped cilantro
1 tablespoon chili powder
2 large cloves garlic, finely chopped
½ teaspoon ground cumin
½ teaspoon salt
1 pound sirloin steak, cut into 2-inch strips
1 small red bell pepper, cut into strips
1 small green bell pepper, cut into strips
1 small onion, sliced
8 (8-inch) ORTEGA Soft Flour Tortillas, warmed
Prepared guacamole

COMBINE salsa, 2 tablespoons vegetable oil, cilantro, chili powder, garlic, cumin and salt in large bowl. Add steak; cover. Marinate in refrigerator for at least 1 hour.

HEAT remaining vegetable oil in large skillet over medium-high heat. Add bell peppers and onion; cook, stirring occasionally for 5 or 6 minutes or until onions are slightly golden and peppers are tender. Add beef mixture; cook, stirring occasionally for 7 to 8 minutes or until meat is no longer pink.

SERVE in tortillas. Top with guacamole.

Bean Fajita

MAKES 3 SERVINGS

2 teaspoons vegetable oil
1 small onion, cut into strips
1 cup red, green and/or
   yellow bell pepper strips
1 can (15 ounces) black,
   pinto or kidney beans,
   drained
½ cup whole kernel corn
1 cup water
1 package (1.25 ounces)
   ORTEGA Fajita
   Seasoning Mix
¼ cup chopped cilantro or
   parsley

6 (8-inch) ORTEGA Soft
   Flour Tortillas, warmed

HEAT vegetable oil in large skillet over medium-high heat. Add onion and bell pepper; cook, stirring occasionally, for 3 to 4 minutes or until vegetables are tender.

STIR in beans, corn, water and seasoning mix. Heat until thickened, stirring often. Remove from heat; stir in cilantro.

SERVE in tortillas.

TIP

Serve fajitas with a radish- and avocado-topped tossed salad.

Mexico's Best Tostada

1¾ cups ORTEGA Refried
    Beans
¼ cup chopped onion
1 package (1.25 ounces)
    ORTEGA Taco Seasoning
    Mix
1 package ORTEGA Tostada
    Shells, warmed
2 cups shredded lettuce
½ cup (2 ounces) shredded
    Cheddar cheese
⅓ cup sliced olives

2 medium ripe avocados,
    cut into 20 slices
¾ cup ORTEGA Thick &
    Smooth Taco Sauce, hot,
    medium or mild

COMBINE beans, onion and
taco seasoning mix in medium
saucepan. Cook, stirring
frequently, for 4 to 5 minutes
or until heated through.

SPREAD ¼ cup bean mixture
over each tostada shell. Top with
lettuce, cheese, olives, avocado
and taco sauce.

NOTE

Making refried beans from scratch would
add hours of preparation time to this recipe.
ORTEGA® Refried Beans add flavor,
without the extra time.

Pulled Pork Tamale

~

4 cups water

2 pounds boneless pork butt or pork roast

1 small onion, quartered

1 teaspoon salt

1 tablespoon vegetable oil

1 cup (1 small) chopped onion

3 cloves garlic, finely chopped

1 cup ORTEGA Diced Green Chiles

1½ to 2 teaspoons ground oregano

Salt and black pepper to taste

COMBINE water, pork, quartered onion and salt in large stockpot. Bring to a boil. Reduce heat to low. Cook, covered, for 1½ to 2 hours or until meat is very tender. Remove pork. Strain broth; reserve ½ cup for meat filling (remaining broth may be refrigerated or frozen for future use). Shred pork.

HEAT oil in large skillet over medium-high heat. Add chopped onion and garlic; cook, stirring occasionally, for 3 to 4 minutes or until onion is tender. Stir in shredded pork, reserved broth, chiles, oregano, salt and pepper. Cook, stirring occasionally, for 4 to 5 minutes or until heat through.

USE filling in burritos, tacos, tostadas or tamales.

Tortilla Lasagna

1 tablespoon vegetable oil

1 to 1½ pounds ground chicken or turkey

1½ cups (2 small) chopped green and/or red bell peppers

1 cup (1 small) chopped onion

1 can (4 ounces) ORTEGA Diced Green Chiles

1 package (1.25 ounces) ORTEGA Taco Seasoning Mix

1 jar (16 ounces) ORTEGA Taco Sauce, divided

10 (8-inch) ORTEGA Soft Flour Tortillas, divided

2 cups (8 ounces) shredded Mexican cheese blend or Monterey Jack cheese, divided

Sliced avocado and chopped cilantro

PREHEAT oven to 375°F. Grease 13×9×2-inch baking dish.

HEAT oil in large skillet. Add chicken; cook, stirring occasionally, until no longer pink. Stir in bell peppers, onion, chiles and seasoning mix. Reduce heat to low; cook, stirring occasionally, until vegetables are slightly tender.

SPREAD ½ cup taco sauce onto bottom of prepared baking dish. Cover with 5 tortillas. Spread with half of chicken mixture and ½ cup taco sauce. Sprinkle with 1 cup cheese. Repeat with remaining ingredients.

BAKE for 15 to 20 minutes or until heated through and cheese is melted. Top with avocado and cilantro.

Mexican Turnovers

¾ cup (about 8 ounces) chopped smoked turkey

¾ cup (3 ounces) shredded Cheddar cheese

1 jar (16 ounces) ORTEGA Salsa, any variety, divided

1 can (4 ounces) ORTEGA Diced Green Chiles

⅓ cup (about 3) sliced green onions

⅓ cup grated Parmesan cheese, divided

1 large egg

2 teaspoons water

1 package (10 ounces) puff pastry shells, thawed

1 tablespoon finely chopped cilantro or parsley

PREHEAT oven to 400°F.

COMBINE turkey, Cheddar cheese, ⅓ cup salsa, chiles, green onions and 2 tablespoons Parmesan cheese in medium bowl. Combine egg and water in small bowl; brush edges of each puff pastry shell with egg mixture.

SPOON ⅓ cup turkey mixture onto half of each shell; fold shells in half over filling. Crimp edges of each turnover with tines of fork. Place turnovers on ungreased baking sheet. Brush with remaining egg mixture; sprinkle with remaining Parmesan cheese and cilantro.

BAKE for 20 to 25 minutes or until golden brown. Serve with remaining salsa.

Veggie-Pepper Bowl with Rice

8 medium green bell peppers, halved and seeded

3 tablespoons water

3 cups cooked long-grain rice

1 package (10 ounces) frozen peas and carrots

1 cup whole kernel corn

½ cup chopped green onions

1¾ cups ORTEGA Salsa, any variety, divided

1½ cups Mexican 4-cheese blend, divided

PREHEAT oven to 375°F.

PLACE bell peppers in microwave-safe dish with water. Cover with plastic wrap. Microwave on HIGH (100%) 4 to 5 minutes, or until slightly tender. Drain.

COMBINE rice, peas and carrots, corn, green onions, ¾ cup salsa and 1 cup cheese in large bowl. Fill each pepper with about ½ cup rice mixture. Place peppers in ungreased 13×9×2-inch baking dish; top with remaining salsa and cheese.

BAKE uncovered for 20 to 25 minutes. Uncover; bake for additional 5 minutes, or until heated through and cheese is melted.

Vegetable Fajitas

1 tablespoon vegetable oil

1 cup (1 small) quartered, sliced onion

1 cup (1 small) red, green or yellow bell pepper cut into strips

1¼ cups black, pinto or kidney beans, rinsed, drained

½ cup whole kernel corn

1 package (1.25 ounces) ORTEGA Fajita Seasoning Mix

⅓ cup water

¼ cup chopped cilantro or parsley

6 (8-inch) ORTEGA Soft Flour Tortillas, warmed

HEAT oil in large skillet over medium-high heat. Add onion and bell pepper; cook, stirring occasionally, for 3 to 4 minutes or until vegetables are tender.

STIR in beans, corn, fajita seasoning mix and water; bring to a boil. Reduce heat to low; cook, uncovered, for 3 to 4 minutes or until mixture is thickened. Remove from heat; stir in cilantro.

SERVE fajita mixture with tortillas.

NOTE

Bursting with bright colors, crisp textures and fresh flavors, this meatless fajita recipe will please everyone—from health-conscious eaters to dedicated meat lovers.

Vegetable Tamales

2 tablespoons vegetable oil

3 cups (3 large) sliced green zucchini

2 cups (2 medium) sliced yellow crookneck squash or yellow zucchini

1 cup (1 small) sliced onion

2 cloves garlic, finely chopped

1 cup (1 medium) chopped tomato

1 cup ORTEGA Diced Green Chiles

½ teaspoon salt

HEAT oil in large skillet over medium-high heat. Add zucchini, squash, onion and garlic; cook, stirring occasionally, for 3 to 5 minutes or until vegetables are tender. Add tomato, chiles and salt; cook for 1 minute or until heated through.

USE filling in burritos, tacos, tostadas or tamales.

Santa Fe Fish Fillets with Mango–Cilantro Salsa

Nonstick cooking spray
**1½ pounds fish fillets
 (cod, perch or tilapia,
 about ½-inch thick)**
**½ package (3 tablespoons)
 ORTEGA Taco Seasoning
 Mix**
**3 ORTEGA Taco Shells,
 finely crushed**
**1 cup ORTEGA Salsa, any
 variety**
½ cup diced mango
**2 tablespoons chopped
 cilantro**

PREHEAT oven to 375°F. Cover broiler pan with foil. Spray with cooking spray.

DIP fish fillets in taco seasoning mix, coating both sides; place on foil. Spray coated fillets with cooking spray. Sprinkle with crushed taco shells.

BAKE 15 to 20 minutes until flaky in center.

MICROWAVE salsa on HIGH (100%) 1 minute. Stir in mango and cilantro.

SPOON salsa over fish when serving.

TIP

Refrigerated jars of sliced mango can be found in the produce section at most supermarkets.

Chili-Chicken Enchiladas

Nonstick cooking spray
3 cups (12 ounces) shredded Cheddar and/or Monterey Jack cheese
1½ cups sour cream
¾ cup roasted red peppers, drained and chopped
1 can (8 ounces) ORTEGA Diced Green Chiles
2 cups diced cooked chicken
1 can (10 ounces) ORTEGA Enchilada Sauce
8 (8-inch) ORTEGA Soft Flour Tortillas

PREHEAT oven to 350°F. Spray 13×9-inch glass baking dish with cooking spray.

RESERVE 1½ cups cheese, ½ cup sour cream and ¼ cup each red peppers and green chiles; set aside.

MIX chicken with remaining cheese, sour cream, red peppers and green chiles in medium bowl.

SPREAD about 2 teaspoons enchilada sauce over each tortilla. Top each with ½ cup chicken mixture. Roll up tortillas; arrange, seam side down, in baking dish.

TOP tortillas with remaining enchilada sauce. Sprinkle with the reserved cheese.

COVER with foil. Bake for 50 to 60 minutes or until hot, removing foil during last 5 minutes of baking time.

SPOON reserved sour cream over top and sprinkle with the reserved red peppers and green chiles.

TIP

Rotisserie chicken is a great time-saver for busy cooks. Try using it for the diced cooked chicken in this recipe.

Dishes

Fiesta-Style Roasted Vegetables

1 can (4 ounces) ORTEGA Diced Green Chiles

3 tablespoons vinegar

2 tablespoons vegetable oil

1 package (1.25 ounces) ORTEGA Taco Seasoning Mix

1 small red bell pepper, cut into strips

1 medium zucchini, cut into ½-inch slices

1 small sweet potato, peeled, cut into ⅛-inch slices and halved

1 small red onion, cut into wedges

Nonstick cooking spray

COMBINE chiles, vinegar, oil and seasoning mix in large bowl; mix well. Add red pepper, zucchini, sweet potato and onion; toss gently to coat. Let stand at room temperature 15 minutes to marinate.

PREHEAT oven to 450°F. Cover 15×10-inch baking pan with foil and spray with cooking spray.

REMOVE vegetables from marinade with spoon, placing on prepared pan.

BAKE 20 to 25 minutes until tender and browned, stirring once.

TIP

Substitute yellow squash for the zucchini, if preferred.

Mexican Hash Brown Bake

Nonstick cooking spray
1 container (13 ounces) ORTEGA Salsa & Cheese Bowl
1½ cups sour cream
1 can (4 ounces) ORTEGA Diced Green Chiles or Diced Jalapeños
1 package (30 ounces) frozen shredded hash brown potatoes
2 ORTEGA Taco Shells, coarsely crushed

PREHEAT oven to 350°F. Spray 13×9-inch baking dish with cooking spray.

COMBINE Salsa & Cheese, sour cream and chiles in large bowl; stir until blended. Gently stir in hash browns. Spoon mixture into baking dish.

SPRINKLE with crushed taco shells.

BAKE for 45 to 50 minutes or until bubbly around edges. Let stand for 5 minutes before serving.

TIP

Make this dish extra special by adding two sliced green onions or two slices crisp, crumbled bacon.

Spicy Skillet Vegetables, Salsa-Style

2 cups finely diced peeled potatoes

½ cup water

2 tablespoons vegetable oil

1 green bell pepper, cut into strips

1 red bell pepper, cut into strips

1 jar (16 ounces) ORTEGA Salsa, any variety

1 can (15.5 ounces) black beans, drained and rinsed

1 can (15 ounces) corn, drained

½ can (¼ cup) ORTEGA Diced Jalapeños

1 cup (4 ounces) crumbled queso fresco or shredded Monterey Jack cheese

MICROWAVE potatoes with water, covered, on HIGH (100%) 5 minutes. Drain. Meanwhile, in large skillet, heat oil over medium-high heat.

COOK and stir bell pepper strips in skillet for 3 to 4 minutes. Stir in drained potatoes and salsa, then beans, corn and jalapeños.

BRING to a boil. Cover; reduce heat to medium and cook for 5 minutes, or until potatoes are tender.

SPRINKLE with cheese before serving.

TIP

If Jalapeños are too hot for your family, use diced green chiles instead.

Salsa-Chili Rice Bake

Nonstick cooking spray
1 cup long-grain rice
1 cup ORTEGA Salsa, any
   variety
¾ cup chicken broth
1 can (4 ounces) ORTEGA
   Diced Green Chiles
½ teaspoon minced garlic
¼ cup shredded Cheddar
   cheese

PREHEAT oven to 350°F.
Spray 1½ quart casserole with
cooking spray.

COMBINE all ingredients
except cheese in large bowl.
Pour into casserole.

BAKE, covered, for 45 to
50 minutes.

SPRINKLE with cheese. Let
stand for 5 minutes.

TIP

A 9-inch baking dish or a 2-quart
casserole may be substituted
for a 1½-quart casserole.

South-of-the-Border Rice and Beans

1¼ cups water

1 cup ORTEGA Salsa, any variety

½ package (3 tablespoons) ORTEGA Taco Seasoning Mix

2 teaspoons vegetable oil

2 cups uncooked instant white rice

1 can (16 ounces) pinto beans, drained and rinsed

¼ cup chopped cilantro

COMBINE water, salsa, seasoning mix and oil in large saucepan; mix well. Stir in rice and beans; mix well.

BRING to a boil over medium-high heat. Cover; remove from heat. Let stand 5 minutes.

STIR in cilantro.

TIP

Serve this side dish with grilled chicken or pork. Brush the meat with oil and sprinkle with extra taco seasoning mix for a flavorful entrée.

Fiesta Potato Salad

LIME JUICE VINAIGRETTE

- ¼ cup lime juice
- ¼ cup olive oil
- ½ teaspoon ground coriander seeds
- ½ teaspoon ground cumin

POTATO SALAD

- 4 medium boiling potatoes
- 1 cup fresh or frozen corn kernels
- 1 to 2 minced ORTEGA Whole Jalapeños
- ½ medium red bell pepper, diced
- ½ medium green bell pepper, diced
- ½ cup finely chopped red onions
- 2 tablespoons chopped cilantro
- Salt and black pepper to taste

WHISK vinaigrette ingredients together in a small bowl. Set aside.

COVER potatoes with water in large pot and bring to a boil over high heat. Lower heat, cover and simmer 25 to 30 minutes, or until tender. Remove from heat, drain and cool slightly. Peel and cut the potatoes into ½-inch to ¾-inch cubes. Cook the corn 2 to 3 minutes, drain and refresh under cold running water.

COMBINE potatoes, corn and vinaigrette in large bowl. Add jalapeños, peppers, onions and cilantro. Season with salt and pepper and mix well. Serve at room temperature or slightly chilled.

Fiesta Corn Bread

2 cups all-purpose flour

1½ cups white or yellow cornmeal

1½ cups (6 ounces) shredded Cheddar cheese

1 can (7 ounces) ORTEGA Diced Green Chiles

½ cup granulated sugar

1 tablespoon baking powder

1½ teaspoons salt

1 can (12 ounces) evaporated milk

½ cup vegetable oil

2 large eggs, lightly beaten

PREHEAT oven to 375°F. Grease 13×9-inch baking pan.

COMBINE flour, cornmeal, cheese, chiles, sugar, baking powder and salt in large bowl; mix well. Add evaporated milk, vegetable oil and eggs; stir just until moistened. Spread in prepared baking pan.

BAKE for 30 to 35 minutes or until wooden pick inserted in center comes out clean. Cool in pan on wire rack for 10 minutes; cut into squares. Serve warm.

Refried Beans Olé

Nonstick cooking spray
2 cans (16 ounces) ORTEGA Refried Beans
½ cup ORTEGA Salsa, any variety
1 can (4 ounces) ORTEGA Diced Jalapeños or Diced Green Chiles
1 cup (4 ounces) shredded Colby & Monterey Jack cheese
4 slices bacon, crisply cooked and crumbled
⅓ cup sour cream (optional)
4 teaspoons chopped cilantro (optional)

PREHEAT oven to 375°F. Spray 2-quart casserole or 9-inch baking dish with cooking spray.

COMBINE refried beans, salsa, jalapeños, cheese and bacon.

SPOON into casserole; cover.

BAKE for 30 minutes or until hot.

TOP with sour cream and cilantro before serving, if desired.

TIP

Substitute ¼ cup cooked bacon bits in place of bacon slices, if desired.

Taco Topped Baked Potato

4 large baking potatoes, scrubbed

½ pound (8 ounces) ground beef

¼ cup chopped onion

1 package (1.25 ounces) ORTEGA Taco Seasoning Mix

1 container (13 ounces) ORTEGA Salsa & Cheese Bowl

Salt to taste

Sour cream (optional)

PRICK potatoes several times with a fork. Microwave on HIGH (100%) uncovered, 12 to 15 minutes or until just tender, turning potatoes over and re-arranging once.

CRUMBLE ground beef into 1 quart glass casserole; add onion. Microwave on HIGH (100%) uncovered, 3 to 3½ minutes or until meat is set, stirring once; drain.

STIR in taco seasoning and half the amount of water specified on taco seasoning package. Add contents of Salsa & Cheese Bowl. Cover. Microwave on HIGH (100%), 2½ to 3 minutes or until heated through, stirring once.

MAKE a crosswise slash in each potato; press side of potato to form an opening. Sprinkle with salt. Spoon filling into potatoes.

TOP each potato with sour cream, if desired.

Soups &

Salads

Hearty Corn, Chili and Potato Soup

MAKES 8 TO 10 SERVINGS

2 tablespoons butter
2 stalks celery, sliced
1 medium onion, coarsely chopped
2½ cups water
2 cups diced potatoes
1 can (14¾ ounces) cream-style corn
1 can (11 ounces) whole kernel corn, undrained
1 can (4 ounces) ORTEGA Diced Green Chiles
2 chicken bouillon cubes
1 teaspoon paprika
1 can (12 ounces) evaporated milk
2 tablespoons flour
Salt and pepper to taste

MELT butter in large saucepan over medium-high heat. Add celery and onion; cook for 1 to 2 minutes or until onion is tender. Add water, potatoes, corn, chiles, bouillon cubes and paprika. Bring to a boil. Reduce heat to low; cover.

COOK, stirring occasionally, for 15 minutes, or until potatoes are tender. Stir a small amount of evaporated milk into flour in small bowl to make a smooth paste; gradually stir in remaining milk. Stir milk mixture into soup. Cook, stirring constantly, until soup comes just to a boil and thickens slightly. Season with salt and pepper.

Black & White Mexican Bean Soup

1 tablespoon vegetable oil
1 cup chopped onion
1 clove garlic, minced
¼ cup flour
1 package (1.25 ounces) ORTEGA Taco Seasoning Mix
2 cups milk
1 can (14 ounces) chicken broth
1 package (16 ounces) frozen corn
1 can (15.5 ounces) great northern beans, drained
1 can (15.5 ounces) black beans, drained
1 can (4 ounces) ORTEGA Diced Green Chiles
2 tablespoons chopped cilantro

HEAT oil in large pan or Dutch oven over medium-high heat. Add onion and garlic; cook until onion is tender.

STIR in flour and taco seasoning mix; gradually stir in milk until blended. Add remaining ingredients except cilantro.

BRING to a boil, stirring constantly. Reduce heat to low; simmer for 15 minutes or until thickened, stirring occasionally.

STIR in cilantro.

TIP

To save time, substitute ½ teaspoon bottled minced garlic for garlic clove.

Mexicali Vegetable Soup

½ pound ground beef
½ cup chopped onion
3½ cups (two 15-ounce cans) beef broth
1 can (14½ ounces) small white beans, drained
1 cup sliced zucchini
1 cup frozen sliced carrots

1 package (1.25 ounces) ORTEGA Taco Seasoning Mix

COOK beef and onion in large saucepan until beef is browned; drain. Add broth, beans, zucchini, carrots and seasoning mix. Bring to a boil. Reduce heat to low; cook, covered, 15 to 20 minutes.

Salsa Chili

1 pound ground beef
1 small onion, chopped
2 jars (16 ounces each) ORTEGA Salsa, any variety
1 can (15 ounces) kidney, pinto or black beans, undrained
1 cup water
1 can (4 ounces) ORTEGA Diced Green Chiles
1 package (1.25 ounces) ORTEGA Taco Seasoning Mix

Sliced green onions, shredded Cheddar or Monterey Jack cheese, diced tomatoes, sliced olives, sour cream and chopped onion (optional)

COOK beef and onion in large saucepan until beef is browned; drain. Stir in salsa, beans, water, chiles and seasoning mix.

BRING to boil. Reduce heat to low; cover. Cook, stirring occasionally for 20 to 25 minutes. Top with green onions, cheese, tomatoes, olives, sour cream and onion, if desired.

Cheesy Mexican Soup

MAKES 8 SERVINGS (1 CUP EACH)

1 cup chopped onion
1 tablespoon vegetable oil
1 container (13 ounces) ORTEGA Salsa & Cheese Bowl
1 can (14 ounces) chicken broth
2 cups milk
1 can (7 ounces) ORTEGA Diced Green Chiles
4 ORTEGA Taco Shells, crushed
¼ cup chopped cilantro

COOK and stir onion in oil in large saucepan over medium-high heat for 4 to 6 minutes until tender. Reduce heat to medium-low.

STIR in Salsa & Cheese, chicken broth, milk and green chiles; cook for 5 to 7 minutes until hot, stirring frequently.

MICROWAVE crushed taco shells on HIGH (100%) 30 to 45 seconds. Cool. Serve soup sprinkled with cilantro and crushed taco shells.

TIP

If you can't find a 7-ounce can of ORTEGA Diced Green Chiles, use two 4-ounce cans.

Zesty Tortilla Soup

1 tablespoon butter or margarine

½ cup chopped green bell pepper

½ cup chopped onion

½ teaspoon ground cumin

3½ cups (two 14½ ounce cans) chicken broth

1 jar (16 ounces) ORTEGA Salsa, any variety

1 cup whole kernel corn

1 tablespoon vegetable oil

6 corn tortillas, cut into ½–inch strips

¾ cup (3 ounces) shredded Mexican blend cheese

Sour cream (optional)

MELT butter in saucepan over medium heat. Add bell pepper, onion and cumin; cook for 3 to 4 minutes or until tender. Stir in broth, salsa and corn. Bring to a boil. Reduce heat to low; cook for 5 minutes.

HEAT vegetable oil in medium skillet over medium-high heat. Add tortilla strips; cook for 3 to 4 minutes or until tender.

LADLE soup into bowls. Top with tortilla strips, cheese and sour cream, if desired.

Mexican Pasta Salad

3 cups (8 ounces) rotini pasta
1 package (1.25 ounces) ORTEGA Taco Seasoning Mix
½ cup sour cream
¼ cup water
1 tablespoon vinegar
1 cup cherry tomato halves
1 can (4 ounces) ORTEGA Diced Green Chiles
½ cup diced green bell pepper
1 can (2.25 ounces) sliced olives, drained
2 green onions, sliced
2 ORTEGA Taco Shells, coarsely crushed
½ cup ORTEGA Salsa, any variety
½ cup (2 ounces) shredded Cheddar cheese

COOK pasta according to package directions (do not overcook); drain. Rinse with cold water until cooled; drain.

STIR together taco seasoning mix, sour cream, water and vinegar in large bowl until blended. Stir in pasta, cherry tomatoes, green chiles, bell pepper, olives and green onions.

MICROWAVE crushed taco shells on HIGH (100%) 30 to 45 seconds.

PLACE pasta in serving bowls. Top with salsa, crushed taco shells and cheese just before serving.

TIP

Stir in a little water for a creamier salad.

South-of-the-Border Salad with Creamy Lime Dressing

CREAMY LIME DRESSING

- ⅓ cup sour cream
- 3 tablespoons chopped cilantro
- 2 tablespoons lime juice
- 1 tablespoon each vegetable oil and milk
- ¼ teaspoon salt

SALAD

- 4 ORTEGA Taco Shells, crushed
- 2 tablespoons vegetable oil
- 1 pound boneless chicken breasts, cut into strips
- 1 package (1.25 ounces) ORTEGA Taco Seasoning Mix
- ¾ cup water
- 1 package (5 ounces) mixed salad greens
- 1 cup cherry tomato halves
- ½ cup ORTEGA Sliced Jalapeños, coarsely chopped
- ½ cup shredded Cheddar & Monterey Jack cheese
- 1 avocado, pitted, peeled, sliced and sprinkled with lime juice

COMBINE all Creamy Lime Dressing ingredients in small bowl; stir until blended.

MICROWAVE crushed taco shells on HIGH (100%) 30 to 45 seconds.

HEAT oil in large skillet over medium-high heat. Add chicken strips; cook and stir 4 to 6 minutes or until chicken is no longer pink. Stir in taco seasoning mix and water. Bring to a boil. Reduce heat to low; cook for 2 to 3 minutes or until mixture is thickened, stirring occasionally. Remove from heat.

COMBINE salad greens, crushed taco shells, tomatoes and jalapeños in large bowl. Divide mixture onto four serving plates.

SPRINKLE each salad with cheese; top with chicken strips and avocado slices.

SERVE with Creamy Lime Dressing.

Smokey Chipotle Salad

1 package (15.2 ounces) ORTEGA Soft Taco Kit

2 tablespoons vegetable oil

¼ cup sour cream

3 tablespoons mayonnaise

2 small chipotle chiles in adobo sauce, seeded and finely chopped

1 pound ground beef

1 bag (15 ounces) romaine salad mix

1 cup (4 ounces) shredded Cheddar & Monterey Jack cheese

1 (2½ ounces) can sliced olives, drained

HEAT oven to 400°F. Brush tortillas from Soft Taco Kit with ¼ teaspoon oil; cut into fourths. Place tortillas on 2 baking sheets. Bake 5 to 7 minutes, or until lightly browned.

PREPARE dressing by combining sour cream, mayonnaise, chipotle chiles and taco sauce from kit; stir until blended.

COOK ground beef as directed on Soft Taco Kit using seasoning mix from kit.

TOSS romaine mix with Chipotle dressing in large bowl until lightly coated.

ASSEMBLE each salad onto serving plates by layering 1½ cups romaine mixture, ⅔ cup beef mixture, 3 tablespoons cheese and 1½ tablespoons olives.

SERVE each salad with tortilla pieces.

TIP

Chipotle chiles in adobo sauce are dried, smoked jalape os in seasoned tomato sauce. They are available in 7- and 11-ounce cans.

Crunchy Mexican Side Salad

3 cups romaine and iceberg lettuce blend

½ cup grape tomatoes, halved

½ cup peeled and diced jicama

¼ cup sliced olives

¼ cup ORTEGA Sliced Jalapeños, quartered

2 tablespoons ORTEGA Taco Sauce

1 tablespoon vegetable oil

⅛ teaspoon salt
Crushed ORTEGA Taco Shells (optional)

TOSS together lettuce, tomatoes, jicama, olives and jalapeños in large bowl.

COMBINE taco sauce, oil and salt in small bowl. Stir with a fork until blended.

POUR dressing over salad; toss gently to coat. Top with taco shells, if desired.

TIP

ORTEGA® Sliced Jalapeños are available in a 12-ounce jar. They are pickled, adding great flavor and crunch to this salad.

Chicken Taco Salad Wraps

1 ripe large avocado, pitted, peeled and diced

¾ cup peeled and diced jicama

2 teaspoons lime juice

2 tablespoons vegetable oil

1 pound boneless chicken breasts, cut into strips

1 package (1.25 ounces) ORTEGA Taco Seasoning Mix

¾ cup water

8 ORTEGA Taco Shells, coarsely crushed

12 large Bibb lettuce leaves

½ cup (2 ounces) shredded Mexican blend cheese

¼ cup chopped fresh cilantro

1 jar (8 ounces) ORTEGA Taco Sauce

STIR together avocado and jicama with lime juice in small bowl; set aside.

HEAT oil in large skillet over medium-high heat. Add chicken strips; cook and stir 4 to 6 minutes or until chicken is no longer pink. Stir in taco seasoning mix and water. Bring to a boil. Reduce heat to low; cook for 2 to 3 minutes or until mixture is thickened, stirring occasionally. Remove from heat.

MICROWAVE crushed taco shells on HIGH (100%) 1 minute.

SPOON ⅓ cup chicken filling onto each lettuce leaf; layer with taco shells, avocado mixture, cheese and cilantro. Wrap lettuce around filling and serve with taco sauce.

Chopped Salad Tostadas

1 package ORTEGA Tostada Shells

6 cups (½ large head) shredded iceberg lettuce

1 cup shredded carrot

1 can (2.25 ounces) sliced olives, coarsely chopped

1 tomato, seeded, chopped and drained

⅓ cup ranch dressing

6 tablespoons ORTEGA Taco Sauce, divided

1 can (16 ounces) ORTEGA Refried Beans

10 tablespoons shredded Mexican blend cheese

HEAT tostada shells according to package directions. Meanwhile, in large bowl, gently toss lettuce, carrot, olives and tomato.

MIX ranch dressing and 2 tablespoons taco sauce in small bowl. Pour dressing over lettuce mixture; toss gently to coat.

COMBINE refried beans and 4 tablespoons taco sauce in saucepan; heat over medium heat until warm.

SPREAD each tostada shell with 3 tablespoons bean mixture; top with ¾ cup salad mixture and sprinkle with cheese.

TIP

Mexican blend cheese is a blend of four types of cheese. You can also use Cheddar or Monterey Jack cheese.

Index

Arroz con Pollo... 36
BBQ Chicken Tacos.. 41
Bean and Cheese Burrito.. 34
Bean Fajita 43

BEEF
  Fajita Celebration 42
  Fiesta Beef Enchiladas 38
  Mexicali Vegetable Soup... 76
  Mexican Pizza 22
  Mexican Steak Tacos 33
  ORTEGA® Fiesta Bake 37
  Puffy Tex-Mex Pillows 20
  Salsa Chili.. 77
  Smokey Chipotle Salad 86
  Taco Topped Baked Potato...................................... 70

Black & White Mexican Bean Soup 74
Breakfast Burritos 14
Breakfast Empanadas 10
Breakfast Tacos.. 10

BURRITOS
  Bean and Cheese Burrito... 34
  Breakfast Burritos.. 14

Cheesy Mexican Soup 78
Chicken Taco Salad Wraps 90
Chili-Chicken Enchiladas... 54
Chile 'n' Cheese Spirals... 18
Chopped Salad Tostadas 92
Crunchy Mexican Side Salad.. 88

ENCHILADAS
  Chili-Chicken Enchiladas... 54
  Fiesta Beef Enchiladas 38

FAJITAS
  Bean Fajita 43
  Fajita Celebration 42
  Vegetable Fajitas 50

Fajita Celebration 42
Fiesta Beef Enchiladas 38
Fiesta Corn Bread... 67
Fiesta Potato Salad... 66
Fiesta-Style Roasted Vegetables.................................... 57
Hearty Corn, Chili and Potato Soup 73
Mexicali Vegetable Soup.. 76
Mexican Hash Brown Bake 58
Mexican Omelette 9
Mexican Pasta Salad... 82
Mexican Pizza 22
Mexican Roll-Ups.. 26
Mexican Steak Tacos... 33
Mexican Tortilla Stacks 17
Mexican Turnovers.. 47
Mexico's Best Tostada 44
ORTEGA® 7-Layer Dip 24
ORTEGA® Fiesta Bake 37
ORTEGA® Hot Poppers... 31

ORTEGA® Nachos.. 30
ORTEGA® Snack Mix 21

PORK
  Breakfast Burritos.. 14
  Breakfast Empanadas 10
  Breakfast Tacos... 10
  Pulled Pork Tamale 45
  Refried Beans Olé 68

POULTRY
  Arroz con Pollo.. 36
  BBQ Chicken Tacos.. 41
  Chicken Taco Salad Wraps 90
  Chili-Chicken Enchiladas.. 54
  Mexican Tortilla Stacks 17
  Mexican Turnovers... 47
  South-of-the-Border Salad with Creamy Lime Dressing..... 84
  Tortilla Lasagna... 46
  Turkey Tacos 40

Puffy Tex-Mex Pillows 20
Pulled Pork Tamale 45
Refried Beans Olé 68

SALAD
  Chicken Taco Salad Wraps 90
  Chopped Salad Tostadas 92
  Crunchy Mexican Side Salad................................... 88
  Fiesta Potato Salad.. 66
  Mexican Pasta Salad.. 82
  Smokey Chipotle Salad 86
  South-of-the-Border Salad with Creamy Lime Dressing... 84

Salsa Chili.. 77
Salsa-Chili Rice Bake.. 62
Santa Fe Fish Fillets with Mango-Cilantro Salsa.............. 52

SEAFOOD
  Santa Fe Fish Fillets with Mango-Cilantro Salsa.............. 52

Smokey Chipotle Party Dip 28
Smokey Chipotle Salad 86

SOUP
  Black & White Mexican Bean Soup.............................. 74
  Cheesy Mexican Soup.. 78
  Hearty Corn, Chili and Potato Soup.......................... 73
  Mexicali Vegetable Soup... 76
  Salsa Chili... 77
  Zesty Tortilla Soup 80

South-of-the-Border Rice and Beans............................... 64
South-of-the-Border Salad with Creamy Lime Dressing.......... 84
Spicy Skillet Vegetables, Salsa-Style............................... 60

TACOS
  BBQ Chicken Tacos.. 41
  Breakfast Tacos... 10
  Mexican Steak Tacos 33
  Turkey Tacos 40

Taco Topped Baked Potato 70
Tortilla Lasagna.. 46
Tortilla Scramble with Salsa 12
Turkey Tacos 40
Vegetable Fajitas 50
Vegetable Tamales... 51
Veggie-Pepper Bowl with Rice 48
Zesty Tortilla Soup 80